YOUR KNOWLEDGE HAS VALUE

Eric Rosenberg

The National Association of Professional Base Ball Player's: The Origins of Professional Baseball and The American Identity

GRIN Verlag

Bibliografische Information der Deutschen Nationalbibliothek:

Die Deutsche Bibliothek verzeichnet diese Publikation in der Deutschen National-
bibliografie; detaillierte bibliografische Daten sind im Internet über http://dnb.d-
nb.de/ abrufbar.

Imprint:

Copyright © 2011 GRIN Verlag GmbH
Druck und Bindung: Books on Demand GmbH, Norderstedt Germany
ISBN: 978-3-656-39418-1

This book at GRIN:

http://www.grin.com/en/e-book/211231/the-national-association-of-professional-
base-ball-player-s-the-origins

GRIN - Your knowledge has value

Der GRIN Verlag publiziert seit 1998 wissenschaftliche Arbeiten von Studenten, Hochschullehrern und anderen Akademikern als eBook und gedrucktes Buch. Die Verlagswebsite www.grin.com ist die ideale Plattform zur Veröffentlichung von Hausarbeiten, Abschlussarbeiten, wissenschaftlichen Aufsätzen, Dissertationen und Fachbüchern.

Visit us on the internet:

http://www.grin.com/

http://www.facebook.com/grincom

http://www.twitter.com/grin_com

"The National Association of Professional Base Ball Players:
The Origins of Professional Baseball and the American Identity"

With almost utmost certainty, the sun will rise in the east, set in the west, and Major League Baseball will begin a new season in the spring. Such has been assured since 1871, as professional baseball first complemented everyday American life by virtue of the National Association of Professional Base Ball Player's (NAPBBP) inaugural season. The formation of the NAPBBP denoted a fundamental separation of amateur and professional baseball clubs, and the eternal intertwining of sport and business. This moment in history would more broadly beget a critical juncture in the development of the modern American identity as this era of the nineteenth century is characterized by a generation of citizens who have only known an autonomous United States, thereby distinguishable as the first purely born and bred American population. With this new status came the need to comprehend what constituted wholly American values beyond just regional, economic, and social distinctions, the remnants of a fractious colonial past. Baseball quickly became part of this new sense of American similitude, labeled the "national pastime" for nearly its entire existence. As baseball grew from a regional game into a nationwide phenomenon, more drastic change accompanied, by means of money permeating the sport. The five seasons of NAPBBP play from 1871 to 1876 transpired during a decidedly dynamic period of American history. The societal identity formation occurring during the early stages of the Gilded Age corresponds both in time, and essence, with baseball's maturation process, culminating in a purely professional NAPBBP. Through analyzing these simultaneous processes, their relation to one another, and the notion of baseball as a microcosm of American society, what characteristics became inherently American, who had the power to actually establish these allegedly universal ideals, and the implications such principles had on the nation's population become apparent. Baseball, and more specifically the NAPBBP, offered the principal values of late nineteenth century collective American society.

Baseball's beginnings, like many of our country's forefathers, can be traced back to England. Emerging from traditional ball-games like cricket and rounders, baseball was part of a movement of young people taking part in outdoor recreational activities as a medium for exercise and social gathering. This new generation of Americans, the ones who would be the first to participate in the national pastime, grew up in the early nineteenth century and lived in an independent America from birth. Baseball's pioneer players lived mainly in the Northeast and unlike their colonial ancestors, who were rightly occupied with erecting a New World civilization and pursuing religious freedom, these young men and boys had time for leisure.[1] Baseball quickly filled this void. By 1845, the first organized club, the New York City's Knickerbocker Club was established as a "fraternal" group of young men playing impromptu intra-squad games, paying little attention to who won or lost the games but instead to promoting health, recreation, and social interaction. By the 1850's, more clubs organized in the New York City area and games between clubs had become commonplace, with competition still in a complementary role to leisure and socializing.[2] As the organized baseball club system continued to grow outwards from New York to new groups of players, this perception of the sport as merely a mode of exercise among friends evolved alongside other changes in American society.

Many of the first formal baseball clubs were organized along professional or geographical lines. Warren Goldstein describes in his book *Playing for Keeps* that "certain clubs were centered in particular trades, workplaces, or neighborhoods" and "the experience of baseball play in the mid-nineteenth century was not very far removed from the experience of work, especially from the world and culture of the urban workplace."[3] This early makeup of baseball clubs reflected the growing significance of industrialization and the city in American society as baseball's rise in popularity occurred during the most extensive period of urbanization in United States history. In 1860, 6.2 million Americans lived in urban areas, or places with 2,500 or more residents. By 1900, this number grew considerably to 30 million people and the number of urban areas nearly quadrupled. Between 1860 and 1880, big cities, or urban areas with a population larger than 100,000 individuals, realized an increase in number from nine to twenty. Most of these new urbanites came by way of migration from rural areas and immigration from foreign countries. These individuals came to cities in pursuit of economic success, for manufacturing was progressively replacing agriculture as the leading industry in the United States during this period.[4] These changes resulted in a contemporary urban environment composed of people with similar jobs and economic status living near one another in dense communities. Many early baseball clubs formed based on these associations, like the Esculapian Club of Brooklyn composed of physicians or the Malta Club that strictly accepted milkmen.[5] Individuals who played baseball, which at this point still retained many of its fraternal elements, teamed up with neighbors and co-workers to play the game as a leisurely escape from the grind of the industrial work. This manner of organization came with several implications that would ultimately alter the role of baseball in these young cities and serve as the origin for the development of professionalism and the NAPBBP.

The increased number of clubs, along with the players' strong sense of loyalty to them, procured leisure and exercise giving way to competition and an opportunity to exude dominance over a rival profession or neighborhood. Now that the results of a game reached beyond the extent of one club playing in isolation of the others, competition progressed from a private to public matter. Losing had consequences that affected a club's reputation, and moreover an identifiable group's perception among others also living in their communities.[6] Clubs began employing a "first nine", or the best nine players on the team, when previously the best players would be split up and play any position to ensure fair teams for intra-squad games. The first nine would practice by playing in the field together against the inferior players of the club to become specialized at a certain position and develop their skills for the now meaningful and competitive inter-club games.[7] Additionally, the heightened emphasis on competition warranted a singular set of rules as to avoid confusion and unfair play.

While many forms of the game existed during the sport's youth, the New York Knickerbockers, the first baseball club, dictated the direction of baseball's style. Known as the "New York Game", these set of rules differed from the other popular approach, the "Massachusetts Game". The "Massachusetts Game" involved no foul territory, a larger field, and "plugging" or using the ball as a weapon to peg the base runner for an out.[8] The "New York Game" became the standard for competitive baseball and accelerated the sport's growth as the game became quicker-paced, thus more exciting for both spectators and players. Baseball's rapid progression into a more widely played, skilled, and defined game compelled the prominent clubs of the time to collaborate and form a National Association of Base Ball Players (National Association). Officials from fourteen New York City and Brooklyn clubs met on January 22nd, 1857 to create a uniform set of rules, agree on a standard ball, collect a $2 entrance fee from each club, and elect officers to govern the organization.[9] This convention symbolized the beginning of formally established and regulated sport leagues in the United States and the first step towards an eventual schism between amateur and professional baseball.

Before proceeding to chronicle the history of the National Association and the ultimate creation of a separate professional league, the NAPBBP, it is crucial to look back on the brief, yet significant, beginnings of baseball and its relationship to the development of the modern American identity. While Mark Twain and Charles Dudley Warner did not coin the term "Gilded Age" until writing their novel *The Gilded Age. A*

Tale of Today in 1874, what was happening in the amateur baseball world up to the National Association's first convention in 1857 foreshadowed the eventual course of events of the society on a national scale and also the small, yet growing, world of professional baseball. "Gilded" is defined as being covered with a thin layer of gold, and while only superficial, light reflecting off the precious metal can amaze the beholder.[10] Such was the case with the emergence of the elite, competitive baseball clubs in the first National Association. While teams like the New York Knickerbockers represented only the minority of baseball clubs, those composed of highly skilled and competitive players, their actions dictated the direction of baseball. Americans were taught that sport was a means for character training and self-discipline, and that the vigor associated with playing baseball made for a better person.[11] However, the masses, which were still dominantly rural, unskilled, and unrefined even amidst industrialization, were emphatically supporting a sport that was steadily becoming more suited for a minority of urbanites, skilled players, and the gentlemanly type. The National Association became the golden standard for the baseball community yet was misrepresentative of average, amateur baseball players. Similarly, urbanization and industrialzation influenced the representation of the opportunistic, rich capitalist as the epitome of American success while in reality the average American still had an agrarian background and little or no ability in industry. Glenn Porter illustrates this divide, "Although the heartland's values retained remarked and disproportionate force despite the shifting economic realities, America's cultural tune was in fact gradually coming to be called more by the urban and industrial sectors and less by the rural and agrarian ones."[12] The introduction of professionalism and the formation of the NAPBBP magnify these issues even more.

Henry Chadwick, like the National Association and New York Knickerbocker Club, is a "gilded" figure in the baseball community, as he had great authority over the direction of the game despite being misrepresentative of the leisurely baseball player or average fan. Before becoming known as the "Father of Baseball", Chadwick, born in Exeter, England on October 5, 1824, grew up playing cricket before moving to New York at the age of twelve. Chadwick soon became fond of baseball and went on to write about the sport in several New York newspapers and magazines as a young man. He would become the sport's greatest promoter, author of its rulebook, and respected authority on all matters baseball. He believed baseball's popularity was due to its apparent compatibility with the national character and also saw professionalism as the natural course of evolution of the game as long as it remained a business void of corruption and gambling.[13] His book, *Chadwick's Base-Ball Manual for 1871*, coincides with the founding of the NAPBBP and also chronicles the history of the National Association beginning with its inception in 1857.

Henry Chadwick's *Chadwick's Base-Ball Manual for 1871* provides much of the history of the National Association and also the sequence of events that resulted in the National Association of Professional Base Ball Players. For the purpose of this paper, *Chadwick's Base-Ball Manual for 1871* will be used both as a secondary source objectively reporting historical facts as well as a primary source that gives insight to his own biases as a heralded figure in the baseball community. Chadwick begins his manual with an introduction remarking on the recent developments in the sport as well as his predictions for the future. Acknowledging that baseball's height of popularity coincides with the beginning of a professional league, Chadwick is very aware of the enormity of the NAPBBP's first season and its place in what would become a lengthy history, "the season's work of 1871, both on the field, and in the clubrooms and convention halls, is to make or mar the future of our national pastime."[14] Amidst the author's comments is an attribution of the beginning of the sport to the year 1860 during the height of amateurism, and not 1845 with the introduction of the first amateur club. By making this distinction, Chadwick seems to assume that professionalism and the NAPBBP was always the direction baseball was headed in. Because he subscribes to the idea that baseball fits American culture and also to the advancement of professionalism, Chadwick believes that professional baseball best suits what he assumes to be the country's identity, one characterized by specialized skilled work centered in urban areas. An amateur team could materialize from nine interested individuals of any skill level in any part of the country; this expression of baseball being available to the vast majority of Americans. However, by maintaining professional baseball as the ultimate manifestation of the sport, he ostracizes the amateur majority as passive spectators of the "true" game played by the professional minority in large urban areas. He chronicles the most transformative moment of baseball's brief history as the National Association's 1864 rule change that made only catching the ball in the air an out, thus removing the "bound catch" or an out made catching the ball off a bounce. At this point the National Association was composed of both professional and amateur teams, but the expulsion of the "bound catch" would so drastically widen the gap in adeptness between the two that coexistence in one league would soon become utterly unfeasible. From Chadwick's perspective, these happenings brought baseball "nearer to the point of perfection" and led to a "real struggle" for the championship.

The growth of the National Association from fourteen teams from New York City in 1857 to over three hundred clubs from twenty-three states and Washington, D.C by 1867 demonstrates how expansive baseball truly was during this time period. Baseball's growing popularity and universality on a national scale ironically was paired with rule changes that made the game harder for the average player. During this ten-year period, representatives from National Association clubs voted to make the ball smaller and lighter, thereby harder to both catch and hit. Additional rules were drafted to make balls caught off a bounce no longer an out and bad pitches warranted a penalty of a "ball" and four balls led to a free base. All of these changes made the game more difficult and better suited for very skilled player. Just like baseball as the American pastime, the "American system" of manufacturing was celebrated during the Gilded. Characterized by high volume production through specialization and strong machinery, the American system of manufacturing received the attention of motivated entrepreneurs trying to capitalize on the country's newfound successes in industry.[15] This American system had a striking resemblance to the emerging professional baseball teams of the same time. With the 1866 ruling by the National Association's officers that baseball players could be paid for their services, clubs entirely composed of professionals began to organize. These teams produced a high level of talented play through signing specialized players who excelled at one position, with pitchers being the most valued for their scarcity and unique skill set. What made both the American system and professional team possible were large amounts of capital. Conversely, small-scale local businessmen and amateur teams could not compete with their immensely more powerful counterparts, despite being in the same industry or playing the same game. Level playing fields did not exist in either case. In baseball's situation, tension amounting from a minority of professionals making the decisions for the National Association led to a split during the 1870 convention.[16] This would signal the end of the National Association incorporating both amateur and completely professional teams, forever changing the identity of competitive sports.

These developments further the argument that baseball was a model for American culture and seemingly provided a resolution to the identity crisis of the time. Moreover, these changes expound the types of individuals that can define these qualities and provide answers to the masses searching for the American way. While the original National Association was composed of hundreds of clubs, with the majority amateur in nature, a minority group of professional club owners dictated the future of baseball and its overall public perception. These individuals' interests culminated in the separation of National Association of Professional Base Ball Players only ten years after the original association of amateur clubs formed in 1857. This rapid and significant schism demonstrates how certain values attain their worth and what forces mold the perceptions of value and meaning. People like Henry Chadwick, with a platform to communicate and an audience to listen, can permeate a minority belief, like professionalism in baseball, into a defining characteristic of the majority held identity. The introduction to *Chadwick's Base-Ball Manual for 1871* is short, yet effectively illuminates this idea. By stating that rule changes that make baseball more difficult and suited more for skilled players are happening concurrently with the sport's height of popularity, Chadwick insinuates that baseball greatness can only be attained by the minority of talented, privileged individuals still able to excel at the sport despite its increasing difficulty. The masses were now being told that the baseball they played, and succeeded in, during their youth was not the "perfect" version of the national pastime. The introduction of professionalism into baseball still allowed it to be enjoyed by the majority, yet only mastered at its highest level by a minority. This shift unveils what might be the true nature of American society during the Gilded Age and potentially even modern society, a continually rising ceiling that thrusts the talented, exceptional few into the spotlight while leaving a growing majority incapable of fulfilling the ultimate definition of success. The American Dream promotes equal opportunity based on work ethic and dedication; however, this dream is realistically limited by an individual's inherent level of skill or intelligence and their family's race, wealth, and reputation. Henry Chadwick and the founders of the NABBP marketed their sport as the "national pastime," an equalizer in which all Americans can participate. Yet, these same advocates steadily and effectively pushed an agenda for professionalism, concretely defining the measure of baseball achievement to no longer be in character or work ethic, but instead dollars and cents.

On March 17, 1871, representatives of professional clubs created the National Association of Professional Base Ball Players. Professional teams developed illustrious reputations after playing inferior amateur teams for years. They achieved perpetual success with their consistently stellar performance on the field, high interest and revenue from fans, and ensuing ability to pay large contracts to maintain the best rosters every season. Hurriedly created without much foresight and employing the same rules drafted for a league of both professionals and amateurs, the NAPBBP only lasted five seasons. This quick rise and fall demonstrates many of the same pitfalls of Gilded Age American society. Because the league only had a $10 entrance fee and no screening process for expansion clubs, teams from small markets like Keokuk, Iowa and Middleton, Connecticut entered the league without any chance of making a profit. High player salaries further destroyed small clubs' ability to compete financially with larger clubs.[17] A tangible divide arose between the league's competitive, wealthy teams and the losing, struggling teams. The lack of competition, evidenced by the Boston Red Stockings winning four of the five championships, led to a declining interest in the NAPBBP and its ultimate termination in 1876. Players leaving teams in pursuit of larger contracts, gambling, a lack of a strong central authority, and scheduling issues also contributed to the leagues ultimate failure. That same year, Chicago White Stockings owner William Hulbert decided to create a new league, the National League. The National League corrected the mistakes the NAPBBP had made by limiting membership, controlling contracts, increasing admission fees, and creating a fixed schedule. Professional baseball did not die with the NAPBBP, as the National League still exists today.[18]

Just as professional baseball proved to be the rule and not the exception, so did industrialization and capitalism as cornerstones of the American identity. However, using the NAPBBP as an isolated circumstance in which professional baseball did fail to some degree illustrates the main failures of the American identity being rooted within the minority of the successful rich. America did not catapult to the top of the global economy without instances of moral shortcomings. Capitalism is inexorably linked to excess, greed, corruption, fraud and bribery, all these especially prominent in the Gilded Age in which industrialization boomed and some would do anything to acquire what they believed to be the American dream.[19] The NAPBBP realized the same inadequacies with small market clubs taking risks entering the league blinded by greed or good players leaving clubs in shambles without a hint of loyalty in pursuit of larger contracts. By the American identity being synonymous with material wealth, and professionalism baseball also being muddled by capitalism and corruption, someone trying to be what they believe to be successful could have easily taken the wrong, immoral path towards the perceived American dream. While professional baseball and American industry have still thrived despite these failures, it may be very possible the masses could have secured a truer sense of American identity, one based on a meritocracy of character and will instead of wealth and possession, had professionalism never been introduced to the sport or industrialization never occurred.

The late nineteenth century population was preoccupied with understanding and procuring a uniquely American success amid vast and rapid changes in the country's economic and social systems. This struggle is evident in the baseball community, specifically among writers grappling with the idea of baseball as a component of the country's identity on par with urbanization and industrialization. As early as the 1850's writers began to refer to the sport at "the national pastime". These writers saw the rapid rise of baseball to a national level as an opportunity to comment on American singularity during a period in which the country remained divided on the slavery issue and how decentralized states can function together with a centralized federal government. An August 26, 1869 article in a New York City magazine, *The Nation*, compared the "truly American game" to its European counterpart cricket. The author characterizes cricket as "an imported invention not suited to the peculiar institutions of the country"[20] and attributes differences between the two sports to divergent national identities. The author believed Americans as a whole were less violent than the English, who use a harder ball in cricket that causes more injuries, as well as enjoy novelty and excitement, evidenced by the faster pace of baseball. Cricket had existed for centuries and had organized leagues with professionals in England; nevertheless, the author compares it to the young, unorganized baseball. While the author probably wrote the article to demonstrate his newfound appreciation for baseball and appeal to readers who were also immersed in the cultural phenomenon, the fact that he felt the need to unify Americans against a common opponent demonstrates the ongoing identity crisis during the late nineteenth century for a singular set of American values. At the time this was published, divisions regarding slavery, states' rights, and the economic direction of the country among others had permeated the population. The core of the struggle was simply defining the right, moral way to live in United States that every citizen could subscribe to, regardless of what state they lived in, what country their ancestors came from, or any other segmentation of the American people. In this particular case, the author believed all Americans could agree on avoiding brutality in leisurely activities and seeking excitement. Although these characteristics are probably true for most populations and are trivial in essence, by drawing a connection between what the author attributes as American values to baseball, a sport that was sweeping the nation, this author was able to feel as if he reconciled the identity crisis of the time.

Judy Hilkey's book *Character is Capital* explicates these same ideas but in the context of the American identity during the Gilded Age. Hilkey focuses on the phenomenon of success manuals beginning around 1870. These manuals guaranteed discouraged, worrisome American men a way to find success in life. Written by educated members of society, this literature was marketed to rural, small-town men, individuals who naturally felt unsuccessful with the ideal American being urban, economical, and wealthy as dictated by the minority industrial class. Selling million of copies in the late nineteenth century, the authors of these manuals believed "character was capital"[21] and honesty, frugality, and loyalty were both the moral guides to success and realization of success itself. Like the baseball writers, and even amateur players of the era, the authors of these success manuals created an ideal identity unable to be attained by those who were supposedly able to. Small-town rural men bought books like these because they felt inadequate for they were always told that powerful capitalists like Rockefeller and Vanderbilt were the epitome of success. Even if they were to become high-character individuals and find relative success on a small-scale, they can still never reach this nearly impossible level of success that the "true" American dream suggests. Similarly, the average baseball of the time, no matter how much practice or passion they had, were limited by their own athletic ability and rampant competition for a limited number of professional jobs. As professional baseball and the NAPBBP made the sport vastly more compatible with a certain minority then the majority, the character of a baseball player was not enough to realize the ultimate vestige of baseball greatness.

The modern American identity formed during the Gilded Age inaccurately represents the average member of the masses. Created by an elite minority, the portrayal of the national character as urban, progressive, and skilled excludes millions of Americans who cannot fulfill this definition of the American dream. Professional baseball and the NAPBBP advanced the same ideals from 1871 to 1876. By promoting professionalism and making money an intrinsic part of the game, the NAPBBP and its leaders effectively ostracized the average, amateur player from achieving baseball greatness while relying on this same individual to consume their product as fans. While capitalism and professional baseball are ardently rooted in our American identity, and also have undoubtedly provided accomplishment and happiness to many people, they represent much of what is flawed in our country and how we define success in it. Major League Baseball has evolved into a multi-billion dollar industry and yet, had money never become part of the game, there may have been a Babe Ruth and Willy Mays in every community, town, or city around the United States. The NAPBBP set the precedent of the baseball greats being not the everyman practicing and enjoying the game for free, but the select few could hit the ball the furthest, throw it the hardest, all while getting paid astronomical amounts for simply partaking in the national pastime. The National Association of Professional Baseball Players laid the groundwork for a thriving professional sports industry in the United States, but in doing so, facilitated the development of an identity unsuitable for the average baseball enthusiast, the universal American, and the common man.

---

[1] William R. Hooper, "Our National Pastime," *Appleton's Journal: A Magazine of General Literature*, February 25, 1871, 225

[2] Tom Melville, *Early Baseball and The Rise of the National League* (Jefferson, North Carolina: McFardland & Company, Inc. Publishers, 2001), 10.

[3] Warren Goldstein, *Playing for Keeps: A History of Early Baseball* (Ithaca, New York: Cornell University Press, 1989), 24.

[4] Robert G. Barrows, "Urbanizing America," in *The Gilded Age,* ed. Charles W. Calhoun (Lonham, Maryland: Rowman & Littlefield Publishers, Inc., 2007), 101-118.

[5] Hooper, "Our National Pastime," 226.

[6] Melville, *Early Baseball and The Rise of The National League,* 10.

[7] Goldstein, *Playing for Keeps: A History of Early Baseball,* 22.

[8] Melville, *Early Baseball and The Rise of The National League,* 11.

[9] Our National Sports," *The New York Herald,* 23 January 1857, B8.

[10] Ruth C. Crocker, "Cultural and Intellectual Life in the Gilded Age," in *The Gilded Age,* ed. Charles W. Calhoun (Lonham, Maryland: Rowman & Littlefield Publishers, Inc., 2007), 211-237.

[11] Ellen M. Litwicki, "The Influence of Commerce, Technology and Race on Popular Culture in the Gilded Age," in *The Gilded Age,* ed. Charles W. Calhoun (Lonham, Maryland: Rowman & Littlefield Publishers, Inc., 2007), 187-209.

[12] Glen Porter, "Industrialization and the Rise of Big Business," in *The Gilded Age,* ed. Charles W. Calhoun (Lonham, Maryland: Rowman & Littlefield Publishers, Inc., 2007), 11-27.

[13] Steven P. Gietschier, "Henry Chadwick," *American National Biography Online,* February 2000. http://www.anb.org.proxy.library.vanderbilt.edu/articles/19/19-00021.html (accessed April 9, 2011).

[14] Henry Chadwick, *Base-Ball Manual for 1871* (New York, New York: America News Company of New York, 1871).

[15] Porter, "Industrialization and the Rise of Big Business," 15.

[16] David Quentin Voight, *American Baseball* (Norman: University of Oklahoma Press, 1966), 35.

[17] Goldstein, *Playing for Keeps: A History of Early Baseball,* 146.

[18] "National Association," *Baseball Chronology,* http://www.baseballchronology.com/Baseball/Leagues/National_Association/ (accessed April 7, 2011).

[19] [15] Porter, "Industrialization and the Rise of Big Business," 12.

[20] "The Philosophy of the National Game," *The Nation,* 26 August 26 1869, 167-168.

[21] Judy Hilkey, *Character is Capital: Success Manuals and Manhood in Gilded Age America* (Chapel Hill and London: The University of North Carolina Press, 1997), 5.

Works Cited

Robert G. Barrows. "Urbanizing America," in *The Gilded Age,* ed. Charles W. Calhoun (Lonham, Maryland: Rowman & Littlefield Publishers, Inc., 2007), 101-118.

Henry Chadwick. *Base-Ball Manual for 1871* (New York, New York: America News Company of New York, 1871).

Ruth C. Crocker. "Cultural and Intellectual Life in the Gilded Age." in *The Gilded Age,* ed. Charles W. Calhoun (Lonham, Maryland: Rowman & Littlefield Publishers, Inc., 2007), 211-237.

Steven P. Gietschier. "Henry Chadwick." *American National Biography Online,* February 2000. http://www.anb.org.proxy.library.vanderbilt.edu/articles/19/19-00021.html (accessed April 9, 2011).

Warren Goldstein. *Playing for Keeps: A History of Early Baseball* (Ithaca, New York: Cornell University Press, 1989).

Judy Hilkey. *Character is Capital: Success Manuals and Manhood in Gilded Age America* (Chapel Hill and London: The University of North Carolina Press, 1997).

William R. Hooper. "Our National Pastime". *Appleton's Journal: A Magazine of General Literature*. February 25, 1871, 225-226.

Ellen M. Litwicki. "The Influence of Commerce, Technology and Race on Popular Culture in the Gilded Age." in *The Gilded Age,* ed. Charles W. Calhoun (Lonham, Maryland: Rowman & Littlefield Publishers, Inc., 2007), 187-209.

Tom Melville. *Early Baseball and The Rise of the National League* (Jefferson, North Carolina: McFardland & Company, Inc. Publishers, 2001).

"The Philosophy of the National Game." *The Nation*, 26 August 26 1869, 167-168.

Glen Porter. "Industrialization and the Rise of Big Business." in *The Gilded Age,* ed. Charles W. Calhoun (Lonham, Maryland: Rowman & Littlefield Publishers, Inc., 2007), 11-27.

National Association." *Baseball Chronology,* http://www.baseballchronology.com/Baseball/Leagues/National_Association/ (accessed April 7, 2011).

David Quentin Voight. *American Baseball* (Norman: University of Oklahoma Press, 1966).